Sentencing, Penal Policy and Management in a Correctional Facility

Kimberley Bartolo

Bibliographic information published by the German National Library:

The German National Library lists this publication in the National Bibliography; detailed bibliographic data are available on the Internet at http://dnb.dnb.de.

ISBN: 9783346308559
This book is also available as an ebook.

© GRIN Publishing GmbH
Nymphenburger Straße 86
80636 München

Print and binding: Books on Demand GmbH, Norderstedt, Germany
Printed on acid-free paper from responsible sources.

The present work has been carefully prepared. Nevertheless, authors and publishers do not incur liability for the correctness of information, notes, links and advice as well as any printing errors.

GRIN web shop: https://www.grin.com/document/958694

Sentencing, Penal Policy and Management in Corrections

Author: Kimberley Bartolo

Table of Contents

Discuss the struggles encountered by correctional managers while formulating policies which are aimed at achieving the following objectives; (i) strengthening the management of staff working within a correctional facility; (ii) ameliorating professional service provision to maintain the holistic wellbeing of inmates; (iii) implementing penal sentences that meet the needs of the offender, the victim and society in general.

Introduction

The word 'policy' is extremely hard to define since it holds different connotations and meanings to everyone (Torjman, 2005). However, a common understanding of the word is about having a set of ideas which are used within a particular organization, in this case being the prison setting, in order to make particular decisions which can influence one's behaviour (Freeman, 1999). When creating a policy, for it to be well structured and maintained, it needs to focus upon delivering its main objectives (Torjman, 2005). The objectives of a prison, revolve around the rehabilitation and reintegration of the prisoner (Gaines & Miller, 2015). Correctional managers are faced with a number of challenges whilst, they are formulating such policies. These struggles are going to be discussed in the following sections.

(i) Struggles in strengthening the management of the Staff working within a Correctional Facility, whilst formulating policies.

Usually, when people talk about prisons, they only mention the physical attributes about them like for example, the locked up building with bars. However, prisons are much more than that (Coyle, 2009). They also consist of the essential roles of the staff working within them, whom have a crucial part in the prisoners' process of reintegration and rehabilitation. In order for the management to be strengthened, all the staff needs to understand their role within the prison, whom they should report to and be able to meet the needs of the service users, i.e. the inmates, society and victims (Magretta & Stone, 2002).

The staff consists of three groups, which are; the civil servants, professionals and the correctional officers. Having three different groups working within the prison, may cause several struggles. This is because they all come from different cultures, and their mentality may vary. Hence, they all look at the clients from different perspectives. Nonetheless, finding the staff whom are adequate to work within the prison is challenging for the correctional manager. The way the staff treats and works with the prisoners, has a major impact on their rehabilitation and reintegration process. So, it is of outmost importance that the staff understands what the prisoner is going through (Saunders, Rosch, Katzenelson, Li & Curtis, 2017). Prison life is different from life outside and so the prisoner is facing various changes in his life. Staff that work within the prison setting need to empathize with the prisoners but, at the same time pose discipline (Coyle, 2009). Imagine that while a prisoner is serving his sentence, his wife leaves him. The prisoner is not only facing the changes that are happening in his environment but, also those happening in his personal life. Therefore, it is crucial for the staff who are working with this prisoner to understand his situation. Yet, this may be difficult at times since, human beings tend to lack empathy towards each other. This is especially evident when the other person is portrayed as being 'evil' and so, the prisoner is seen as deserving what has happened to him (Witchalls, 2011). Thus, rather than employing someone with the mind-set of a military person, one needs to employ someone whose point of view is similar to that of a social worker since they are capable of being empathic but at the same time pose the necessary discipline. Lastly, in order for the staff to be adequate, they should all have clear views on what their role is. Correctional managers need to provide a clear guide for each staff in which the roles are clearly explained (Criminal Justice Handbook Series, 2010).

Additionally, the role of each prison staff should be supported by others. However, this proves to be challenging as well since there is poor management. There is a lot of division and distrust amongst each of the staff (Authority, 2009). According to varies research, certain staff like the correctional officers, are not appreciated by others (Authority, 2009; Howard League, 2017). They are not seen as being professionals. This can be highly demotivating for them since, they feel undervalued and are seen as having a role which is not as important. Generally speaking, all prison staff suffer from a 'status'. They are not valued as much as other people working within the criminal justice field, like for example the police (Coyle, 2009). This is all evident from the low salaries that they have and also from the lack of training opportunities that they are offered. All these factors, reduce the willingness for adequate staff to want to work within the prison setting. For this reason, it is very hard for the correctional manager to find qualified people whom are willing to work within the prison (Coyle, 2009).

Training is also a challenging task for the correctional manager. Not just providing it financially but also, due to staff shortage. The latter, is a challenge within itself, but it is even more of a challenge when the small number of staff working in a prison were to be taken away for training- whom would there be left to take care of the prisoners whilst the staff are being trained? (Howard League, 2017). This is a major concern, as when staff lacks other problems arise one of which being, prison safety (Savage, 2018). So, the issue is upon who should be trained and when should it be provided. Consequently, if the staff stops receiving training, other challenges would arise such as, burnout (Youmans, 2013). Considering that the opportunity to progress in one's role is not given, due to lack of training, the staff would stop giving their utmost in the job and would start to feel dis-incentivized as, they would not be able to progress which will make them lose all the enthusiasm in the job (Mulligan, 2015; Savage, 2018). One way to avoid this from happening is by rewarding the staff with incentives and ranks. This will not only keep them motivated to work hard but also reduce burnout. In fact, Howard League for Penal Reform (2017), stated that prison officers "need different grades of officers" (p. 6), which means that someone with years of experience should not be regarded the same as someone who has just started, or else it will reduce the willingness for the more experienced staff to keep working in that job (Savage, 2018). Nevertheless, rewarding the staff can also be a challenging task. How would correctional managers provide such incentives for its staff? If, for example, correctional managers were to provide flexible hours for its staff as part of an incentive, there can be occasions in which the prison is less secure than others due to having lack of staff during those hours.

Moreover, a challenge that is faced by every staff working within the prison is lack of resources and space. Most of the prisons that are still being used today were built over a century ago. In the past, prisons were focused on punishing the inmates rather than rehabilitating and reintegrating them. Thus, they were not structured in a way to provide the necessary space and resources for staff to carry out their services. For example, psychologists find it hard to deliver sessions with the inmates due to the lack of space; while other staff, like for instance doctors, may lack resources that they need to be able to work properly (Blackburn, Fowler, & Pollock, 2014; Van Ginneken, 2016).

(ii) Struggles in ameliorating professional service provision to maintain the holistic Wellbeing of inmates, whilst formulating policies

It can be very hard to identify who the professionals are, and even harder to explain who truly is considered as being one (Dall 'Alba, 2009). One way to identify professionals, is through warrants and level of education that they have. However, this is not a simple task for correctional managers. It is not just about finding people with warrants and PHDs. It is also about choosing what type of professionals should be employed. In order for the holistic wellbeing of an inmate to be maintained, the biopsychosocial approach has to be used. This approach looks at the prisoner from the biological, psychological and social perspective (Frankel, Quill & McDaniel, 2003). This means that correctional managers would need to employ professionals that fall under all three of the perspectives. This can be challenging for a number of reasons.

Firstly, is the biological perspective. This perspective focuses on the prisoner living a healthy lifestyle, rather than simply the absence of illnesses. Most times, a person leading a criminal lifestyle does not prioritize his health, especially drug addicts. It is important to have professionals that do not simply look at the crime that the prisoner has committed but, who also look at the circumstances which led to the crime (Frankel et al., 2003; Clarkson, 2005; Scott & Codd, 2010). So, who are the professionals that should be employed from this perspective? Primarily, they should be those that provide primary health care services, such as nurses and doctors. This is a challenge though, as prisoners are classified according to their needs. This means that each classification of prisoners would need their own nurses, for instance. If, one prisoner has taken drugs due to being influenced by a friend, he is going to need different treatment than someone who is taking drugs to cope with a personal problem. They are both considered as drug abusers however, there reasons vary. Nurses, need to understand this difference between the prisoners, in order to be able to maintain properly their overall wellbeing and help them understand how to live a healthier life.

Secondly, is the psychological perspective. This focuses upon understanding what the prisoner is feeling and thinking, which results in his behaviour (Frankel et al., 2003). Its focus lays upon the repressed issues from one's past. For instance, if the prisoner that was taking drugs due to a personal problem never spoke about his issues, then they become suppressed. In this case, the most relevant professionals to work with the prisoner would be psychologists. According to Haag (2006), a psychologist working within the prison setting has a fundamental role in the reintegration and rehabilitation of a prisoner. One challenge in this area would be finding psychologists whom are willing to work within the prison setting. The prison has its own environment, psychologists that are going to work with prisoners need to be able to work within that environment, follow prison policies and its culture. This can be challenging since the professional might not feel at place (Broomfield, 2018). Thus, it is hard to find psychologists whom are willing to work in the prison setting. Also, another challenge is that sometimes, those psychologists that decide to work in a prison setting do not fully do it because they are truly concerned with rehabilitating and reintegrating the prisoner, but look at it as being a career opportunity (Martin, 2008). Therefore, the correctional manager should be cautious about whom to employ.

Thirdly, is the social perspective which looks at the social factors, such as interactions with others, that can have an influence on the person's overall wellbeing (Gove, 1994). Amongst other professionals that should be employed under this perspective, are social workers. As DeVeaux (2014), alludes the aim of a social worker is to "enhance human wellbeing and help meet the basic needs of people" (p. 106). Yet, finding such professionals whom are willing to work with prisoners is challenging for different reasons. One reason being that of the clashes between the values that a social worker has and that the criminal justice system has (Toi, 2015), which as a result makes it hard for the social workers to do their job. A prison values control and order whilst, social workers value human relationships, amongst other things. Thus, they are faced with several ethical dilemmas and role conflicts, which makes it hard for them to work within such a setting (Toi, 2015). For this reason, it is extremely challenging to find social workers willing to work within prisons. Social workers do not only work with the prisoner's themselves, but also their families. This is because their families also need to learn how to cope with the changes that occurred in their lives due to the imprisonment (Ronald, 2011).

Every professional needs to be capable of working hand-in-hand with other professionals and also other staff that are working within the prison.

(iii) Struggles in implementing penal sentences that meet the needs of the Offender, the Victim and Society, whilst formulating policies

Imprisonment of a prisoner will not only impact him but also the other two systems, i.e. the victim and society. This is why the needs of all three systems need to be considered when implementing penal sentences. In order to do so the theory of restorative justice needs to be implemented as it focuses on repairing the damage done by a crime on all systems (Johnstone & Van Ness, 2011).

Firstly, is the prisoner himself. Treating each and every prisoner in humane ways is a must. All prisoners are still human beings, and so they need to enjoy their human rights. When people are imprisoned they lose their right for free movement; but this does not mean that their basic human rights are lost as well, such as the right to contact their family. This is not just a right for the prisoners but also for the family members (Barnard, 2007; Coyle, 2009). Correctional managers are responsible to ensure that such rights are developed and maintained. Penal sentences should be equal to all offenders, and should not pose any form of discrimination (European Prison Rules, 2006). According to the Nelson Mandela Rules (United Nations, 2015), each and every prisoner should be treated with dignity and no form of discrimination should take place when it comes to sentencing. However, this is not always the case. When compared to white males, black men are at a higher risk of facing imprisonment (Tonry, 2012). The prison population in Malta consists of a diversity of inmates, coming from all around the world and from different cultures. Correctional managers should be familiar with diversity, so that the right policies are implemented and avoid any form of discrimination (Branigin, 2018).

Furthermore, another challenge faced by correctional managers is coming up with the behaviours that should be considered as being criminal, and the amount of time they should get as a penal sentence. For instance, does criminalizing drugs make it less attractive for the offender (Gruber, n.d.)? Not really, because if this were to be the case the number of drug convictions would be lower and prison populations would also be lower. Such crimes not only harm the prisoner himself but also bring social harm within communities (Khalooei, Mashayekhi-Dowlatabad, Rajabalipour & Iranpour, 2016). Hence, the penal sentences implemented should always keep in mind the affects it will have on all three systems.

Secondly, is the victim. Frequently, victims of a crime tend to be forgotten as the attention is focused on the offender- "I was treated like a piece of 'trash', while the offender received all of the attention" (Wemmers, 1996, p.1). Penal sentences should also meet the needs of victims, which include; financial and emotional needs (Wemmers, 1996). There are several challenges faced by correctional managers within this area like for example, how are prisoners supposed to recompense for their crime in order for it to be enough to satisfy the victim? With the length of the penal sentence? Most prisons are over-crowded and so, crimes which occur a lot (such as drug-related crimes) tend to not be penalized as harshly so as, to avoid over-crowding in prisons. Because of this, victims feel that their needs are not being prioritised (Ghosh, 1992) and that the offender is basically running away with hurting them. Open prisons were also created as a way to avoid over-crowding in prisons. How safe does the victim feel knowing that their offender is still running around within the community (Ghosh, 1992)? On one hand, correctional managers do not want over-crowding to occur since it is dangerous for prisons, while on the other, they do not want to be seen as not giving importance to victim's needs.

Lastly, are the needs of society. Societies argue that giving the offender a longer prison sentence, is not going to stop the offender from re-offending. They also argue that community sentences are more effective at reducing crime (McDowell, 2012). Societies have the right to expect that offenders are effectively rehabilitated and reintegrated (MacCormick, 1950). However, this can also be challenging for the correctional managers to tackle as it is not just society whom he has to consider but the other two systems as well. Do victims feel safe if prisoners where to carry out community sentences rather than prison ones? Are the prisoners themselves safe to be around their victims and in society? Community service is a way of showing that prisoners still care about society, and that they regret the damages that they have done. In fact, in order for the prisoners to make up for some of these damages, prisoners in the Maltese prison, decided to come up with a play which shows how much they are willing to change. One of the prisoners also stated that they are often portrayed as being bullies, so with this kind gesture they can give something back to society which will hopefully make them look better (One News Malta, 2014). This plays a role in the rehabilitation process.

Furthermore, communities are not always willing to accept former prisoners back. In fact, challenges faced by prisoners, which have to do with their re-integration process, are; employment, housing and labels. Due to being labelled and having a criminal record, employers are not willing to employ them which makes it hard for ex-prisoners to find a job. Consequently, they are not able to become financially independent (Bushway, Stoll & Weiman, 2007), which results in the ex-prisoner not being able to pay for accommodation and housing.

Conclusion

In conclusion, correctional managers have an important role within the prison system. As discussed above, such managers are faced with many challenges which need to be tackled on a daily basis so that, the prison setting is able to reach its main objectives, that of rehabilitating and re-integrating the prisoners. Without their role, such objectives would not be reached. Hence, it is important to acknowledge all the responsibilities that correctional managers have and understand all the work that is put into formulating policies.

References

Authority of the House of commons. (2009). Role of the prison officer [PDF file]. *House of Commons Justice Committee.* Retrieved from https://publications.parliament.uk/pa/cm200809/cmselect/cmjust/361/361.pdf

Barnard, M. (2007). *Drug addiction and families.* Retrieved from https://books.google.com.mt/books?id=e-4PBQAAQBAJ&printsec=frontcover&dq=families+with+a+drug+user&hl=en&sa=X&v ed=0ahUKEwirj93_67DfAhUFEiwKHeWaCKoQ6AEIJzAA#v=onepage&q=families %20w ith%20a%20drug%20user&f=false

Blackburn, A. G., Fowler, S. K., & Pollock, J. M. (Eds.) (2014). *Prisons: today and tomorrow* (3rd Ed.). Retrieved from https://books.google.com.mt/books?id=MbRZRJmWbXQC&pg=PR15&dq=lack+of+ re sources+in+prisons&hl=en&sa=X&ved=0ahUKEwj4pMaY4-3fAhUJiCwKHashB_0Q6AEIQzAF#v=onepage&q=lack%20of%20resources%20in %20p risons&f=false

Branigin, A. (2018, December 19). First step is one of the biggest criminal justice reforms in decades. But how great will its effects be? *The Root.* Retrieved December 21, 2018 from https://www.theroot.com/first-step-is-one-of-the-biggest-criminal-justice- refor-1831214003

Broomfield, K. (2008). *Challenges psychologists encounter working in a correctional setting* (Master's thesis). Retrieved from Campus Alberta http://dtpr.lib.athabascau.ca/action/download.php?filename=gcap/Broomfield-Challenges%20Psychologist%20Encouter08.pdf

Bushway, S., Stoll. M. A., & Weiman, D. F. (Eds.) (2007). *Barriers to reentry?: The labor market for released prisoners in post-industrial America.* Retrieved from https://books.google.com.mt/books?hl=en&lr=&id=YOeFAwAAQBAJ&oi=fnd&pg= PR 7&dq=barriers+to+reentry&ots=SrnKDYizRo&sig=jxlJmLqNZZcJYzO5K5RttErNlP Y&red ir_esc=y#v=onepage&q=barriers%20to%20reentry&f=false

Clarkson, C. M. V. (2005). *Understanding Criminal Law* (4th Ed.). London: Sweet and Maxwell Ltd.

Coyle, A. (2009). *A human rights approach to prison management: handbook for prison staff* (2nd ed.). United Kingdom, UK: International Centre for Prison Studies.

Criminal Justice Handbook Series. (2010). Handbook for prison leaders: a basic training tool and curriculum for prison managers based on international standards and norms [PDF file]. *Criminal Justice Handbook.* Retrieved from https://www.unodc.org/documents/justice-and-prison-reform/UNODC_Handbook_for_Prison_Leaders.pdf

Dall 'Alba, G. (2009). *Learning to be professionals.* Retrieved from https://books.google.com.mt/books?id=t0HDAyLUPwUC&pg=PA37&dq=profession al s?&hl=en&sa=X&ved=0ahUKEwiMoo6SmKffAhXLMywKHby8Dj0Q6AEINTAC# v=onep age&q=professionals%3F&f=false

DeVeaux, M. (2014). "Criminal" justice social work in the United States: fulfilling the obligation of social work. *Journal of Law and Criminal Justice, 2*(1), 105-115. Retrieved from https://www.researchgate.net/publication/303298906_Criminal_Justice_Social_Wor k_in_the_United_States_Fulfilling_the_Obligation_of_Social_Work

European Prison Rules. (2006). European Prison Rules. Retrieved from

https://rm.coe.int/european-prison-rules-978-92-871-5982-3/16806ab9ae

Frankel, R. M., Quill, T. E., & McDaniel, S. H. (2003). Introduction to the biopsychosocial approach. In Frankel, R.M., Quill, T. E., & McDaniel, S. H (Eds.), *The biopsychosocial approach: Past, present, future.* Retrieved from https://books.google.com.mt/books?id=hplwZAWGjcMC&printsec=frontcover&dq= biopsychosocial+approach&hl=en&sa=X&ved=0ahUKEwixge3EnqffAhVOqaQKHe NIA 50Q6AEIJzAA#v=onepage&q=biopsychosocial%20approach&f=false

Freeman, R. M. (1999). *Correctional organization and management: Public policy challenges, behaviour, and structure.* United States of America, USA: Butterworth Heinemann.

Gaines, L. K., & Miller, R. L. (2015). *Criminal justice in action* (5th ed.). United States of America, USA: Cengage Learning.

Ghosh, S. (1992). *Open prisons and the inmates* (1st ed.). Mohan Garden, New Delhi: K. M. Rai Mittal for Mittal Publications.

Gove, W. R. (1994). Why we do what we do: a biopsychosocial theory of human motivation. *Social Forces, 73*(2), 363-394. Retrieved from https://doi.org/10.1093/sf/73.2.363

Gruber, C. (n.d.). 5 challenges facing criminal justice professionals right now. *Northeastern University college of professional studies.* Retrieved December 22, 2018 from

https://cps.northeastern.edu/blog/story/5-challenges-facing-criminal-justice- professionals-right-now

Haag, A. M. (2006). Ethical dilemmas faced by correctional psychologists in Canada. *Criminal Justice and Behaviour, 33*(1), 93-109. Retrieved 18 December, 2018 from https://journals.sagepub.com/doi/10.1177/0093854805282319

Howard League for Penal Reform. (2017). The role of the prison officer [PDF file]. *The Howard League for Penal Reform.* Retrieved on December 17, 2018 from https://howardleague.org/publications/the-role-of-the-prison-officer/

Johnstone, G., & Van Ness, D. W. (2011). The idea of restorative justice. In Johnstone, G., & Van Ness, D. W. (Eds.), *Handbook of restorative justice,* pp. 1- 23. Retrieved from https://books.google.com.mt/books?id=U2UQBAAAQBAJ&printsec=frontcover&dq = restorative+justice&hl=en&sa=X&ved=0ahUKEwjloPvc-O3fAhVIDuwKHWtpCr4Q6AEIMTAC#v=onepage&q=restorative%20justice&f=fal se

Khalooei, A., Mashayekhi-Dowlatabad, M., Rajabalipour, M. R., & Iranpour, A. (2016). Pattern of substance use and related factors in male prisoners. *Addiction and health, 8*(4), 227- 234. Retrieved from https://www.ncbi.nlm.nih.gov/pmc/articles/PMC5554802/

MacCormick, A. (1950). The prison's role in crime prevention. *Journal of criminal law and criminology, 41*(1), pp. 36-48. Retrieved from https://scholarlycommons.law.northwestern.edu/cgi/viewcontent.cgi?article=3752 &context=jclc

Magretta, J., & Stone, N. (2002). *What management is: How it works and why it's everyone's business.* Retrieved from https://books.google.com.mt/books?id=iRoRE0HoPbgC&printsec=frontcover&dq=w hat+is+management&hl=en&sa=X&ved=0ahUKEwj0jcK1ru3fAhWGBiwKHT-LAewQ6AEIJzAA#v=onepage&q=what%20is%20management&f=false

Martin, S. (2008). A prison psychologist: McLearen provides or oversees individual and group therapy, drug-treatment services, client assessments, crisis intervention and employee-assistance programs. *American Psychological Association, 39*(4), p. 67. Retrieved from https://www.apa.org/monitor/2008/04/job-prison.aspx

McDowell, P. (2012, July 16). Longer prison sentences are not the way to cut crime. *The Guardian.* Retrieved December 22, 2018 from https://www.theguardian.com/commentisfree/2012/jul/16/longer-prison- sentences-civitas

Mulligan, D. (2015). *Stress, burnout and coping strategies among prison officers serving in the Irish prison service* (Bachelor's thesis). Retrieved from Dublin Business School (DBS) https://esource.dbs.ie/handle/10788/2791

One News Malta. (2014. April 8). *Ħabsin fi sforz biex jagħtu xi ħaġa lura lill-vittmi tagħhom* [Video file]. Retrieved December 20, 2018 from https://www.youtube.com/watch?v=9sP2lnqaT_8&fbclid=IwAR3_-rbsLCaA8Js0gw0Yq6i579bcJ31tbwLNLrJR37UJW8hbRkflANq76rw

Ronald, Y. (2011). Social work intervention with prisoners: the case of VARHARD in Maharashtra. *Rajagiri Journal of Social Development, 3*(1&2), 99-108. Retrieved from

https://www.researchgate.net/publication/233862396_SOCIAL_WORK_INTERVEN
TI ON_WITH_PRISONERS_THE_CASE_OF_VARHAD_IN_MAHARASHTRA

Saunders, C., Rosch, J., Katzenelson, S., Li, M., & Curtis, S. (2017). Improving staffing and
security in North Carolina Prisons: A review of nationwide prison management
practices [PDF file]. Retrieved from
https://files.nc.gov/ncdps/documents/files/17.12.07%20FINAL_Crime%20Commissi
o
n%20Prison%20Report_0.pdf?fbclid=IwAR3JcBsiPHDQndu_a8BWZ59eZxER3Nn8
Mua WvorXZGaxAlfoGAurMxeyGTE

Savage, M. (2018, April 29). Loss of experienced staff leaving prisons unsafe: jails have lost
officers with 70, 000 years of experience between them in the past decade. *The
Guardian.* Retrieved December 17, 2018 from
https://www.theguardian.com/society/2018/apr/28/loss-experienced-staff-leaves-
prisons-unsafe

Scott, D., & Codd, H. (2010). *Controversial issues in prisons.* England, Berkshire: Open
University Press.

Toi, H. (2015). Professional values and conflict among social workers in prisons: an
examination of role stress, strain, and job satisfaction in working with inmates with
mental illness and/or substance use disorders (Doctoral Dissertation). Retrieved
December 19, 2018 from UCONN Library
https://opencommons.uconn.edu/cgi/viewcontent.cgi?article=7218&context=disser
tations

Tonry, M. (2012). Race, ethnicity and punishment. In Petersilia, J., & Reitz, K. R. (Eds.), *The
Oxford handbook of sentencing and corrections* (pp. 53-82). New York, N.Y.: Oxford

Torjman, S. (2005). What is policy? [PDF file]. Retrieved on December 5, 2018 from

https://maytree.com/wp-content/uploads/544ENG.pdf

United Nations Standard minimum rules for the treatment of prisoners (the Nelson Mandela
Rules). (2015). Retrieved from https://www.unodc.org/documents/justice-and- prison-
reform/GA-RESOLUTION/E_ebook.pdf

Van Ginneken, E. F. J. C. (2016). The pain and purpose of punishment: a subjective
perspective [PDF file]. *Howard league: what is justice?* Retrieved December 4, 2018
from https://howardleague.org/wp-content/uploads/2016/04/HLWP-22-2016.pdf

Wemmers, J. A. M. (1996). *Victims in the criminal justice system.* Retrieved from
https://books.google.com.mt/books?id=rxXP53yNJVMC&printsec=frontcover&dq=h
ow+are+victims+affected+by+penal+sentences&hl=en&sa=X&ved=0ahUKEwib3Y
G9- bDfAhUI1ywKHSG1CBwQ6AEIJzAA#v=onepage&q&f=false

Witchalls, C. (2011, April 5). Why a lack of empathy is the root of all evil. *The independent.*
Retrieved December 6, 2018 from https://www.independent.co.uk/life-style/health-
and-families/features/why-a-lack-of-empathy-is-the-root-of-all-evil-6279239.html

Youmans, A. (2013). Effective Prison management: An international collaboration. *The Corinthian, 14*(2), pp. 1-18. Retrieved from https://kb.gcsu.edu/cgi/viewcontent.cgi?referer=https://www.google.com/&httpsredir=1&article=1041&context=thecorinthian

YOUR KNOWLEDGE HAS VALUE

- We will publish your bachelor's and master's thesis, essays and papers

- Your own eBook and book - sold worldwide in all relevant shops

- Earn money with each sale

Upload your text at www.GRIN.com
and publish for free